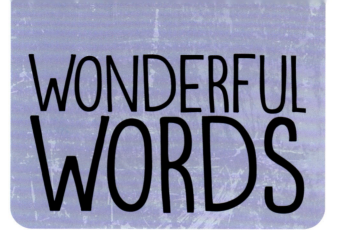

WONDERFUL WORDS

At Home!

First published in 2020 by Miles Kelly Publishing Ltd
Harding's Barn, Bardfield End Green, Thaxted, Essex, CM6 3PX, UK

Copyright © Miles Kelly Publishing Ltd 2020

This edition printed 2021

2 4 6 8 10 9 7 5 3

Publishing Director Belinda Gallagher
Creative Director Jo Cowan
Designer Venita Kidwai
Production Jenny Brunwin
Image Manager Liberty Newton
Reprographics Stephan Davis
Assets Lorraine King

ISBN 978-1-78989-116-4

Printed in China

British Library Cataloguing-in-Publication Data
A catalogue record for this book is available from the British Library

Made with paper from a sustainable forest

www.mileskelly.net

WONDERFUL WORDS

At Home!

Illustrated by Zoe Waring

Miles Kelly

Kitchen

This is where food is cooked.

coffee
machine

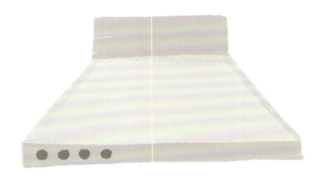

cooker

recycling
bin

drawers

5

Most kitchens have useful machines.

The fridge keeps food fresh.

fridge

toaster

dishwasher

microwave

kettle

Dining room

This is where meals are eaten – breakfast, lunch and dinner.

fruit bowl

beaker

bowl

spoon

high chair

chair

Meals are served on plates or in bowls.
Drinks are poured into cups and glasses.

salt and
pepper pots

cup

saucer

teaspoon

jug

glass

cereal bowl

plate

fork knife spoon

cutlery

What is on the dresser?

dresser

Living room

This room is warm and cosy. You can read a book or relax on the sofa.

cushion

sofa

foot stool

armchair

rug

picture

cactus

pot

vase

ornament

fireplace

Can you spot a spiky plant?

13

A laptop can help with homework.
Then it's time for some TV.

light bulb

lampshade

laptop

keyboard

lamp

table

television

television
cabinet

gaming
console

What do you
like watching
on TV?

remote
control

Utility room

Let's wash some clothes. Once they're dry, ironing smoothes the creases.

Can you spot a red sock?

washing liquid

washing machine

fabric softener

16

17

Everyone can help to keep the house clean and tidy.

bucket

I am cleaning the floor with a mop.

mop

vacuum cleaner

dustpan
and brush

rubber gloves

duster

I reach up high
to dust away
the cobwebs!

sponge

cleaning
spray

19

Playroom

It's fun to share toys when you play with friends.

cuddly toy

toy box

jack in the box

digger

ball

train

rocking horse

building blocks

How many carriages is the train pulling?

marbles

play tent

21

It's fun to paint or draw a picture about a favourite story.

I'm drawing pictures with crayons.

paper

crayon

picture

desk

world map

storybook

easel

picture

paintbrush

paints

I'm painting a picture of my house!

picture book

23

Bathroom

Having a bath before bedtime is a lovely way to finish the day.

bubble bath

shampoo

sponge

towel

shower

I can splash in the bath!

rubber duck

taps

bath

Brush your teeth twice a day.
Always wash your hands after
using the toilet.

tap

toothbrush
holder

soap

toothbrush

plug

toothpaste

sink

How many
toothbrushes
can you count?

toilet

handle

hairbrush

toilet seat

toilet roll

27

Bedroom

Your room is a place to sleep, and keep clothes and toys.

What do you dream about at night?

teddy bear

bed

bunk beds

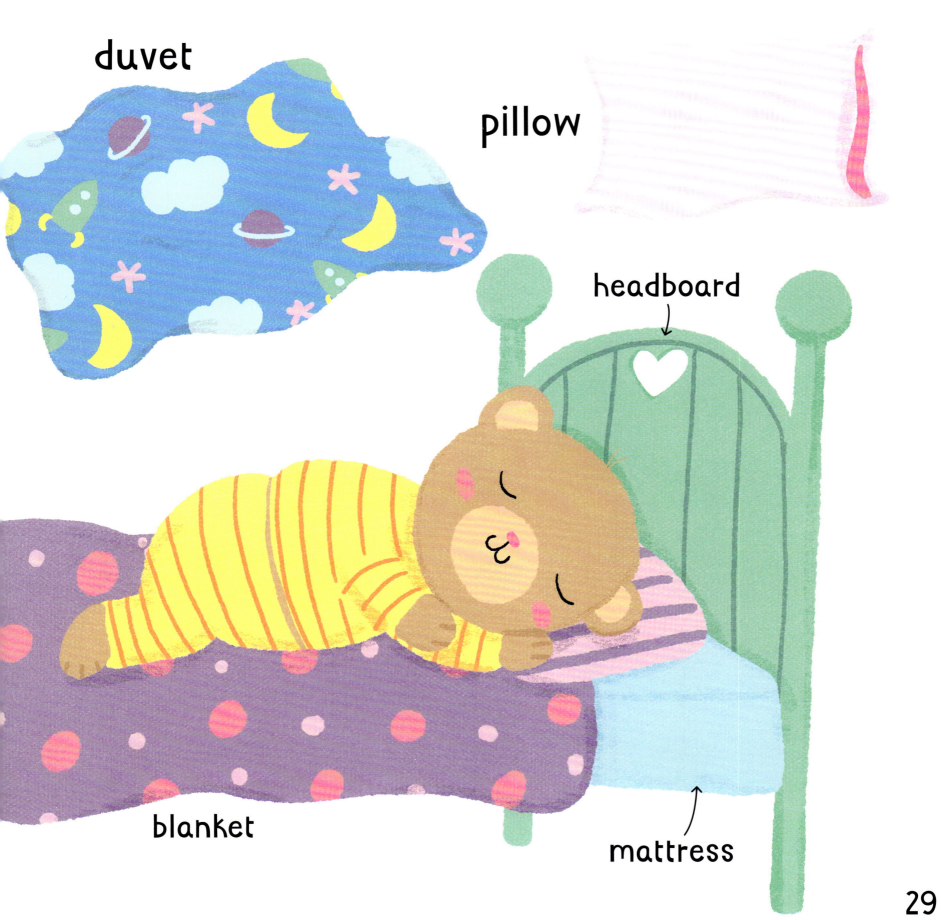

duvet

pillow

headboard

blanket

mattress

29

Do you have a favourite book?

books

lamp

picture

bookshelf

Do you have a favourite toy?

globe

toy box

drawers

window

curtains

coathanger

clothes

wardrobe

dress

socks

shoes

Garden

Let's play in the garden. Washing can be hung out to dry there too.

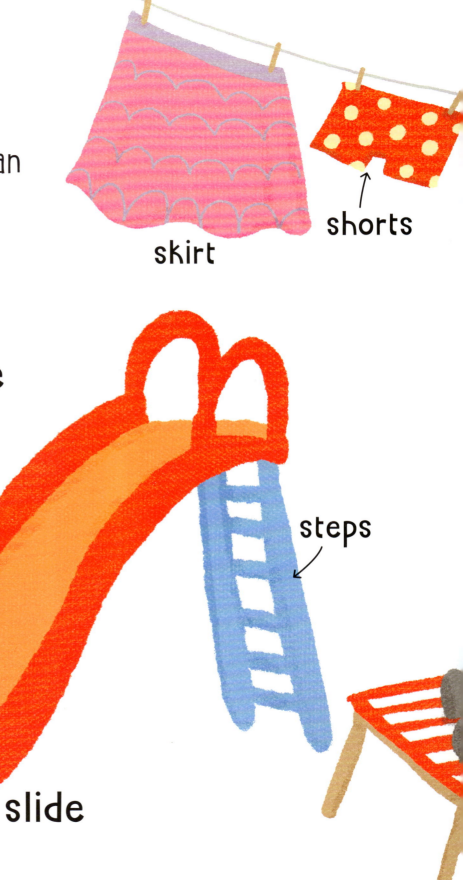

skirt

shorts

flower

fence

grass

slide

steps

washing

peg →

pants

t-shirt

sock

jeans

What games do you like to play outside?

trampoline

sun lounger

33

The garden needs to be kept neat and tidy too.

shed

hosepipe

Can you spot a buzzy bee?

leaves

wheelbarrow

watering can

hanging basket

spade

trowel

fork

flower pot

gardening gloves

lawn mower

35

Garage

This is where a car is kept. It's also a good place to store a bike or a motorbike.

car

I keep my car in the garage at night.

motorbike

handlebars

light

saddle

wheel

pedal

bicycle

Tools are used to fix and make things.

tins of paint

paintbrush

oil can

How many nails can you count?

screwdriver

spanner

stool

nails

workbench

saw

stepladder

vice

hammer

tool box

39

Outside my house

Your home has an outside too!

I think the windows need cleaning!

satellite dish

window

gate

garage

chimney

roof

tree

shutter

conservatory

front door

wall

bench

lawn

steps

3

41

What is your home like?

People live in different types of homes all across the world. Is your house here?

My cottage is small with a roof made of thatch.

log cabin

cottage

bungalow

house

I live in a house built with bricks.

apartments

43

Perhaps your home looks like one of these?

lighthouse

igloo

Could you build a shelter out of snow?

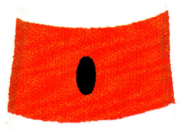

house boat

motor home

castle

treehouse

caravan

mobile home

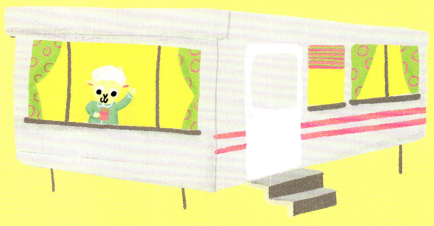

45

Numbers

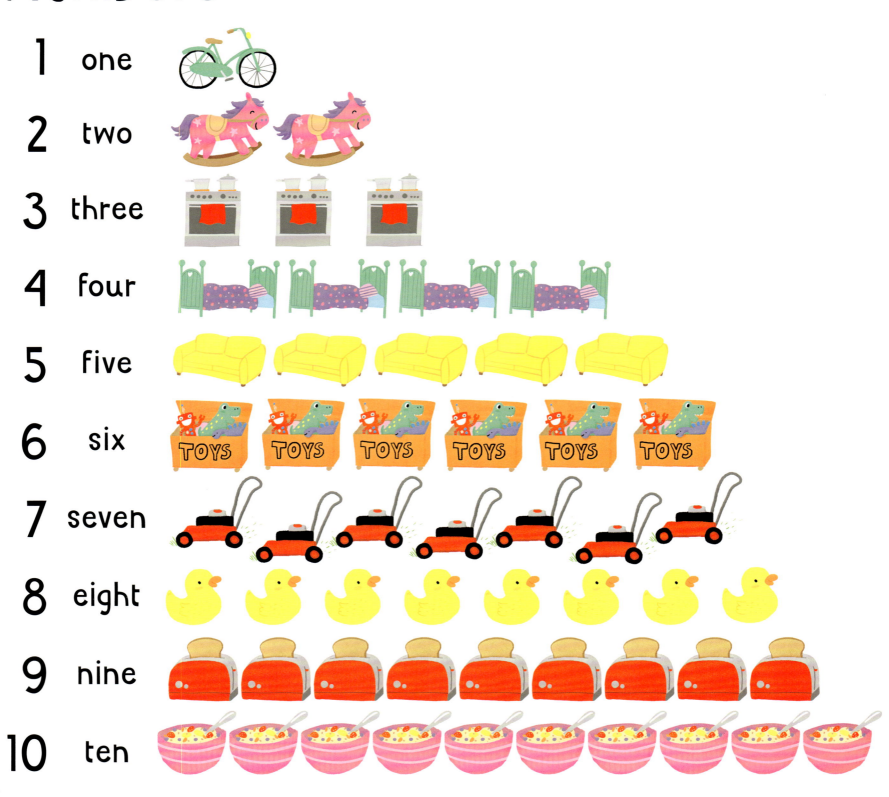

1 one

2 two

3 three

4 four

5 five

6 six

7 seven

8 eight

9 nine

10 ten

11 eleven

12 twelve

13 thirteen

14 fourteen

15 fifteen

16 sixteen

17 seventeen

18 eighteen

19 nineteen

20 twenty

Colours

purple
cuddly toy

yellow
clock

green
lamp

grey
washing
machine

brown
shed

pink
bowl

orange book

black bath

white
fridge

blue
vacuum cleaner

red kettle

48